In the Footsteps of Explorers

Radisson & des Groseilliers

Fur Traders of the North

Katharine Bailey

Crabtree Publishing Company

www.crabtreebooks.com

Crabtree Publishing Company

www.crabtreebooks.com

For my mum, Leslie Bailey, for all of her invaluable help.

Coordinating editor: Ellen Rodger
Series editor: Carrie Gleason
Project editor: Rachel Eagen
Editors: L. Michelle Nielsen, Adrianna Morganelli
Design and production coordinator: Rosie Gowsell
Cover design and production assistance: Samara Parent
Art direction: Rob MacGregor
Scanning technician: Arlene Arch-Wilson
Photo research: Allison Napier

Consultant: Hudson's Bay Company Heritage Services

Photo Credits: Bibliotheque des Arts Decoratifs, Paris, France, Archives Charmet/Bridgeman Art Library: p. 11 (bottom); Bibliotheque Nationale, Paris, France, Giraudon/Bridgeman Art Library: p. 8 (top); British Museum, London, UK/Bridgeman Art Library: p. 23 (top); Cleveland Museum of Art, OH, USA/Bridgeman Art Library: p. 14; Hudson Bay Company, Canada/Bridgeman Art Library: p. 26 (both); Peabody Essex Museum, Salem, Massachusetts, USA/Bridgeman Art Library: p. 20 (top); Yale Center for British Art, Paul Mellon Collection, USA/Bridgeman Art Library: p. 15; Bettmann/Corbis: p. 20 (bottom); Kevin Fleming/Corbis: p. 31; Lowell Georgia/Corbis: p. 29; Leonard de Selva/Corbis: pp. 16-17; Hudson's Bay Company: p. 17 (coat of arms) Trade-mark is the property, and reproduced with the permission, of Hudson's Bay Company; Mary Evans Picture Library / The Image Works: p. 21; Monika Adamczyk/istock International: p. 8 (bottom); Norman Pogson/istock International: p. 28 (top); Rudi Wambach/istock International: p. 24 (middle); Nancy Carter/North Wind Picture Archives: p. 7 (top left); North Wind Picture Archives: p. 5 (bottom), pp. 6–7, p. 12 (bottom left), p. 13, p. 22 (bottom), p. 23 (bottom), p. 25, p. 27, p. 28 (bottom); Other images from stock photo cd.

Illustrations: Colin Mayne: p. 4 (both); David Wysotski: pp. 18-19

Cartography: Jim Chernishenko: title page, p. 10

Cover: Radisson and des Groseilliers traveled in canoes that were large enough to carry cargoes of furs back to New France.

Title page: Radisson and des Groseilliers discovered rivers and mapped trade routes that led to the creation of the Hudson's Bay Company.

Sidebar icon: The Native peoples of North America hunted moose for their meat and soft hides. Radisson and des Groseilliers probably traded for clothing made of moose leather, but they were mostly interested in trading for black beaver pelts.

Crabtree Publishing Company

www.crabtreebooks.com   1-800-387-7650

Cataloging-in-Publication Data

Bailey, Katharine, 1980-
 Radisson and des Groseilliers : fur traders of the north / written by Katharine Bailey.
 p. cm. -- (In the footsteps of explorers)
 Includes bibliographical references and index.
 ISBN-13: 978-0-7787-2422-3 (rlb)
 ISBN-10: 0-7787-2422-0 (rlb)
 ISBN-13: 978-0-7787-2458-2 (pb)
 ISBN-10: 0-7787-2458-1 (pb)
 1. Radisson, Pierre Esprit, ca. 1636-1710--Juvenile literature. 2. Des Groseilliers, Médard Chouart, sieur, b. 1618--Juvenile literature. 3. Explorers--Canada--Biography--Juvenile literature. 4. Explorers--France--Biography--Juvenile literature. 5. Hudson Bay Region--Discovery and exploration--Juvenile literature. 6. Fur trade--Hudson Bay Region--History--17th century--Juvenile literature. 7. Hudson's Bay Company--History--17th century--Juvenile literature. 8. Canada--History--To 1763 (New France)--Juvenile literature. 9. Indians of North America--Canada--History--17th century--Juvenile literature. I. Title. II. Series.
 F1060.7.B35 2006
 971.01'63092--dc22

 2005035760
 LC

**Published in
the United States**
PMB 16A
350 Fifth Ave.
Suite 3308
New York, NY
10118

**Published
in Canada**
616 Welland Ave.
St. Catharines
Ontario, Canada
L2M 5V6

**Published in the
United Kingdom**
White Cross Mills
High Town, Lancaster
LA1 4XS
United Kingdom

**Published
in Australia**
386 Mt. Alexander Rd.
Ascot Vale (Melbourne)
VIC 3032

Contents

Coureurs de Bois

Pierre-Esprit Radisson and Médard Chouart des Groseilliers were French explorers and fur traders. Their discoveries led to the creation of the Hudson's Bay Company, or HBC, Canada's oldest corporation and one of the oldest merchant companies in the world.

New France and Beyond

Radisson and des Groseilliers lived in New France, a French colony in the present-day province of Quebec, Canada. They were *coureurs de bois*, a French phrase which means "runners of the woods." The term described unlicensed fur traders, or men who did not have permission to leave their colonies to hunt animals for their furs.

Fur Trading

Radisson and des Groseilliers wanted to find new places to hunt for beaver pelts. Beaver fur was very valuable in Europe, where it was used to make felt hats. Radisson and des Groseilliers traveled by canoe to Lake Superior and to the upper Mississippi and Missouri rivers, where no Europeans had been before. They traded for furs with local Native groups.

Radisson (left) and his brother-in-law des Groseilliers (right) established new fur trading routes in northern Canada. No known portraits showing what des Groseilliers looked like exist today. These paintings were created by a modern-day illustrator.

The Feast of the Dead

Fur traders often relied on Native peoples who knew the land to guide them through the wilderness. Traders sometimes stayed with these people during the harsh, cold winters of the North. Radisson's journal describes their arrival at a Saulteur village. They arrived at the beginning of a great celebration called the Feast of the Dead, when many Native groups gathered to honor their dead ancestors.

"We arrived at the village by water, which was composed of a hundred cabins without pallasados [palisades, or surrounding walls]. We destinated [gave] three presents, one for the men, one for the women, and the other for the children, to the end that they should remember that journey, that we should be spoken of a hundred years after... The first present was a kettle, two hatchets, and six knives and a blade for a sword, the kettles was to call all nations that were their friends to the feast which is made for the remembrance of the death. That is, they make it once in seven years; it's a renewing of friendship."
-Pierre-Esprit Radisson

(right) Native peoples bringing beaver pelts to the French.

-1618-

Des Groseilliers is born.

-1636-

Historians believe Radisson is born.

-1670-

The Hudson's Bay Company charter is signed.

The French Settlement

New France was a large French colony located along the St. Lawrence River. Samuel de Champlain, an explorer from France, began colonizing the region in 1608, when he founded a settlement called the Habitation of Quebec. New France was a fur trading post, a place where pelts were bought, sold, and prepared for shipping to Europe.

Trading for Furs

New France's economy depended on the fur trade. Champlain and his men traded with the Wendat peoples, who they called the Huron. The Huron brought furs to New France from peoples further north, and traded the furs with European settlers for metal knives and **hatchets**. These items were valued by the Native peoples, who made their tools from rock or clay.

Rivalries

Living in the **New World** was dangerous and difficult. Colonists from different countries in Europe often built settlements side by side. Conflicts occurred between settlers over the land and resources. In 1629, hostilities broke out between the English and the French. The English captured New France and kept it under their control. The Treaty of St. Germain-en-Laye returned New France to the French.

(background) The French helped defend the Huron against their Haudenosaunee, or Iroquois, enemies in the mid-1600s. Wars between the Huron and the Iroquois left the French without furs to trade in Europe.

Unrest

The fur trade was another source of conflict for settlers in the New World. The Huron peoples were long-time enemies with the **five-nation** Haudenosaunee peoples, who the Europeans called the Iroquois. Hostilities between the two groups increased when the European settlers arrived. The French traded with the Huron and sided with them against the Iroquois in a war that began in 1645. The Iroquois defeated the Huron in 1649. After the war, the Huron peoples moved away, died, or were absorbed into other groups. This meant they were no longer the main trading partners for the French, and New France lost its main source of income. At this time, *coureurs de bois* began hunting further northwest, and traded directly with the peoples who lived there, such as the Cree peoples.

(above) Beaver pelts were sent to Europe and sold. The Dutch, English, and French all fought for control over the fur trade in North America.

-1632-

The Treaty of St. Germain-en-Laye is signed, returning New France to the French.

-1686 to 1693-

Pierre le Moyne d'Iberville leads a campaign to capture Hudson Bay's Company trade posts for the French.

-1756-

The Seven Years War between France and England begins.

Young Adventurers

Little is known about Pierre-Esprit Radisson's early life. Historians believe he was born in France in 1636. He moved to New France with his family, where he lived in a village called Trois-Rivières, or Three Rivers.

(left) Historians are not sure why some Iroquois captured European children. They might have been held for ransom. The Iroquois could demand hunting territory in exchange for the release of the captives.

Kidnapped

As a teenager, Radisson was kidnapped during a hunting expedition and held captive by the Iroquois. Radisson spent many months living with the Iroquois as a prisoner. He was adopted by an Iroquoian family who taught him their language, customs, and ways of life. He escaped once, but was found and tortured by the Iroquois. They pulled out his fingernails one by one and drove a red-hot dagger through his foot.

(right) Des Groseilliers' name comes from the French word for gooseberries.

Another Escape

Radisson escaped again in 1653. He went to a Dutch trading post called Fort Orange. He then sailed back to Europe and after a short time, he returned to Trois-Rivières. Later, he joined a **mission** as an interpreter to the land of the Onondaga, a Native group who were members of the Haudenosaunee, or Iroquois Confederacy, in present-day New York.

Young Médard des Groseilliers

Médard Chouart was born in France in 1618. His parents ran a farm called Les Groseilliers. He moved to the Quebec settlement when he was 23 years old, and worked with **Jesuit** missionaries. Missionaries were religious men who traveled to Native communities to **convert** the people there to **Christianity**. After his work with the Jesuits, des Groseilliers moved to Trois-Rivières and married Radisson's half sister. He was also granted land, or a seigneury, which he named after his family's farm in France. **Habitants** helped him farm the land.

The First Expedition

Des Groseilliers learned the Algonquian and Iroquoian languages while working with the Jesuits and travelling to Native communities. This helped him communicate with the peoples he hoped to convert. In 1654, des Groseilliers joined a fur trading expedition with the Huron peoples. They traveled south from Montreal to Lake Huron, and then west to Lake Michigan. The expedition was a success. It returned to Montreal with a **flotilla** of 50 canoes. Each canoe was full of furs for sending to Europe.

(background) On his first mission, des Groseilliers was a lay assistant, or a helper who had not been ordained by the church.

The Partnership

By the late 1650s, New France's fur trade was in ruins because of fighting between the Huron and Iroquois peoples. The French settlers needed to find a new source for furs to keep the colony alive.

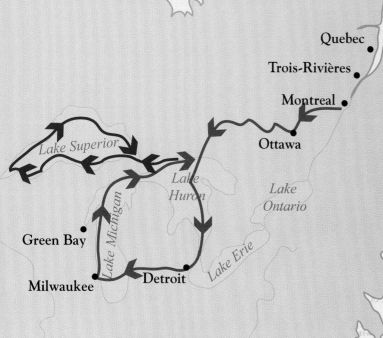

Quebec

Trois-Rivières

Montreal

Ottawa

Lake Superior

Lake Huron

Lake Michigan

Lake Ontario

Green Bay

Milwaukee

Detroit

Lake Erie

NORTH AMERICA

Des Groseilliers' voyage 1654: →→→

Des Groseilliers and

Radisson's voyage 1659-1660: →→→

Forced to Farm

The governor of New France, Pierre Voyer d'Argenson, forbade the settlers from leaving the colony to trade for furs. He wanted the Native peoples to bring furs directly to New France. The governor wanted the settlers to stay in the colony and farm the land so that the community would have enough food to survive the winter months.

Abandoning the Colony

A group of Saulteur peoples came to Trois-Rivières to trade. They agreed to let Radisson and des Groseilliers accompany them back to their village on the southwestern shore of Lake Superior. Together, Radisson and des Groseilliers defied the governor's orders. They stole away in the dead of night with one boat and a stash of weapons and provisions.

(left) On his first expedition, des Groseilliers heard stories about the beautiful beaver furs north of Lake Superior. His request to search for these furs was denied by Governor d'Argenson.

First Leg of the Journey

Radisson, des Groseilliers, and the flotilla of canoes paddled west until they reached present-day Georgian Bay. They entered the strait linking the bay to Lake Superior and followed the southern shore of the lake. The forests along the shore were full of wildlife, which they hunted and killed for food. The winter was fast approaching, so they continued their journey to the village of the Saulteur.

The Fort at Chequamegon Bay

The flotilla reached present-day Wisconsin, where Radisson and des Groseilliers discovered a bay called Chequamegon. They decided to build a small fort while the Saulteur traveled ahead to their village to ensure it had not been attacked in their absence, and to prepare the community for the arrival of their European guests. It is believed that this was the first time the Saulteur villagers had seen white men.

(right) Soon after their journey began, Radisson and des Groseilliers met a band of Iroquois peoples. In his journal, Radisson claims that he and the Saulteur tortured and killed ten Iroquois peoples.

-1654-

Des Groseilliers joins a fur trading expedition with the Huron peoples.

-August 1659-

Radisson and des Groseilliers join a group of Saulteur and travel back to their village.

-1660-

Radisson and des Groseilliers return to Montreal.

Winter in the North

Radisson and des Groseilliers reached the Saulteur village to find great commotion. They exchanged gifts with the Saulteur, giving them metal knives, sewing needles, and axes. They stayed in the village until winter arrived.

Famine

Radisson and des Groseilliers joined a small group to hunt in the forest for the winter. Heavy snowfall made hunting difficult and a famine, or time of hunger, began. Radisson and des Groseilliers almost starved. They ate plants and boiled tree bark. They also ate the dogs they had brought along, and boiled the bones for soup. Many Saulteur died of starvation.

(right) Native peoples made their own weapons, such as tomahawks, from animal bones.

Feast of the Dead

Radisson and des Groseilliers survived the hunting trip and attended the Feast of the Dead, a ceremony in which Native peoples from many communities gather to honor their dead. It is celebrated every ten years. The Cree joined the Saulteur for the celebration and made peace with the Dakota, a people from the same region, who the French referred to as the Sioux. After the feast, Radisson and des Groseilliers visited a Dakota village to trade, then headed to the northern shores of Lake Superior to trade with the local Cree peoples. In his journal, Radisson wrote that he and des Groseilliers traveled up to Hudson Bay at this time, but historians do not believe that they traveled that far north.

(above) Europeans traded metal tools for large quantities of beaver furs.

(left) Before the arrival of Europeans, Native peoples made knives from pieces of wood and chunks of sharp flint.

Back to Montreal

Radisson and des Groseilliers returned to Montreal in the summer of 1660. They traveled in a flotilla of 100 canoes. The canoes were filled with beaver pelts and were paddled by Native peoples. Radisson and des Groseilliers expected a grand welcome when they returned to New France, because they brought furs that would help the colony's economy.

A Hostile Welcome

The men returned to New France with a huge quantity of furs, which would amount to a modern-day value of approximately $350,000. Governor Pierre Voyer d'Argenson promptly confiscated the cargo, and fined them for having left the colony without permission. He also placed des Groseilliers in jail for a short time.

Salvation for New France

Historians believe that the furs Radisson and des Groseilliers brought back saved the colony, which had been on the brink of failure due to the ruined fur trade after the Huron-Iroquois war. The sale of furs in France brought in much needed income. Radisson and des Groseilliers felt betrayed by their governor.

(left) Coureurs de bois *faced many dangers in the wilderness, such as starvation and cold.*

Success in Hudson Bay

The expedition around Lake Superior strengthened the explorers' belief that a valuable fur trade could be established up North. They wanted to sail into Hudson Bay from the Atlantic Ocean and build trading posts along the way, from which they could trade for furs with the local Cree peoples.

New France Refuses

The new trade route would avoid the interior of Canada. Traveling the interior was risky because it included Iroquois territory. Radisson and des Groseilliers asked the governor for permission to seek a northern fur-trading route to Hudson Bay, but they were refused. The governor felt the proposal would **divert** the fur trade further north, which would mean lost territory and profits for New France.

Finding New Partners

Determined to see their vision realized, Radisson and des Groseilliers made a bold move and left New France. They went south to **New England** to ask for funding for their business venture. There, they were told to go to England to seek funds from King Charles II. Radisson and des Groseilliers knew that they would be considered **traitors** if they began trading in the service of the English.

Company of Adventurers

In England, Radisson and des Groseilliers met with King Charles II in 1666. The king agreed to support them. He gave them a **salary,** and introduced them to people who could sponsor their voyage. Prince Rupert, the Duke of Cumberland and Earl of Holderness, organized a group of sponsors, or private **investors** to fund the expedition. The group of investors was later called the Company of Adventurers.

(left) England's King Charles II supported Radisson and des Groseilliers in setting up a new fur trading route.

England Invests

Radisson and des Groseilliers left for England in late 1665. England had just suffered an epidemic of disease that killed thousands. In less than a year a great fire would destroy most of London. Many wealthy English people were looking for new business opportunities. Large merchant companies such as the **East India Company** had proven that overseas trading ventures were profitable. Some English became hopeful that an expedition to Hudson Bay would bring back a wealth of beaver pelts and revive the British economy.

(background) After an epidemic of disease, a fire burned England's capital to the ground. The wealthy began looking for new investing opportunities.

The Expedition

Preparations began for the voyage to Hudson Bay. The Company of Adventurers acquired two ships for the expedition, the *Nonsuch* and the *Eaglet*. The ships were stocked with provisions and set sail from Gravesend, England. Des Groseilliers traveled aboard the *Nonsuch*, captained by Zachariah Gillam. Radisson sailed aboard the *Eaglet,* captained by William Stannard.

The Adventurers Set Sail

The *Eaglet* encountered bad weather shortly after leaving England, so Radisson and his crew were forced to turn back. Des Groseilliers continued on aboard the *Nonsuch*, and reached the coast of present-day Labrador, in the Canadian province of Newfoundland, after two months at sea. They sailed into Hudson Strait and arrived at a site they named Rupert River, after their **benefactor**, Prince Rupert. They constructed a fort called Charles Fort, which was later called Rupert House. It included a house, a cellar for beer and meat, and a stockade, or place where guns and ammunition were housed.

(background) Traders portaged, or took their canoes out of the water to get around obstacles such as waterfalls.

At Rupert River

Des Groseilliers' previous experience in fur trading helped the group develop relations with the local Native peoples. He instructed Gillam, the captain, to establish a League of Friendship with the Cree peoples from James Bay. The League of Friendship was a local tradition, which established an official trading partnership between groups.

Homecoming

Radisson and des Groseilliers wintered in Canada and returned to England the following fall with a large cargo of furs. The voyage did not turn a profit, because the costs of the journey outweighed the sale of the furs. Radisson and des Groseilliers had proven that a fur trading expedition into Hudson Bay was possible, which satisfied the investors.

Hudson's Bay Company

The next year, King Charles II signed a royal **charter** establishing the Hudson's Bay Company (HBC). It gave the Company of Adventurers a trade **monopoly** over the entire drainage basin of Hudson Bay, which became known as Rupert's Land. Radisson's and des Groseilliers' dreams of becoming wealthy fur traders were coming true.

(right) An early version of the Hudson's Bay Company coat of arms featured a fox, two elk, and four beavers.

PRO PELLE CUTEM

-June 3, 1668-

The *Nonsuch* and the *Eaglet* depart England for Hudson Bay.

-June 14, 1669-

The *Nonsuch* sails back to England from Rupert River.

-May 2, 1670-

King Charles II signs the Hudson's Bay Company royal charter.

Life at Sea

The *Nonsuch* and the *Eaglet* were two-masted ships called ketches. The *Eaglet* was leased from the Royal Navy for a fee, while the *Nonsuch,* a former naval vessel, was purchased from a private owner.

Food

The ships' cargo included food that was supposed to last the duration of the two-month voyage, and to carry them through the winter as well. Some of their food items included malt for the ship's beer, lemon juice to ward off scurvy, biscuits, raisins, prunes, peas, oatmeal, sugar, spices, salt beef and pork, wine, and brandy.

Rations

The crew were allotted eight pints of beer daily, as drinking water was limited. Fresh water was kept in wooden casks. During long voyages, a layer of scum called algae grew on the water, making it undrinkable. Beer and wine lasted much longer. The meat was salted to preserve it for longer periods, and spices were brought along to flavor the meat when it started to go bad.

(below) Foods were chosen for their ability to last long periods without refrigeration. Peas were dried and then boiled before they could be eaten. Lemons, full of vitamin C, helped to ward off scurvy, a common seafaring illness. Scurvy resulted from a lack of vitamin C in the diet, caused by a lack of fresh fruits and vegetables.

WINE

Wild Rice

The Native peoples of the Great Lakes region harvested and ate a grain called wild rice. Radisson wrote in his journal that he and des Groseilliers ate wild rice at the Feast of the Dead.

Ingredients:

2 cups (475 ml) wild rice (cooked)
1/2 cup (120 ml) dried cranberries
1/2 cup (120 ml) celery

Directions:

1. Place the cooked wild rice in a large bowl. The rice can be hot or cold.
2. Chop the cranberries and add to the rice.
3. Chop the celery and add to the rice mixture.
4. Stir together and serve.

(right) A sextant was used to measure the height of celestial bodies, or stars and planets, above the ocean. This helped explorers determine their position at sea.

(right) A compass was used to determine the course, or direction in which the ship traveled. A needle pointed North, the direction of the Earth's magnetic pole.

(background) Sleeping quarters on the Nonsuch and the Eaglet were tight. The crew slept in small bunks that were crowded tightly to the sides of the ship below deck. If there were not enough beds, crew members slept on the deck. They slept in shifts, as watchmen, navigators, and other crew members were required day and night.

Ships

The *Nonsuch* was the only ship on the expedition to make it to Hudson Bay, as the *Eaglet* was forced back to England by a storm. The *Nonsuch* weighed 45 tons (41 tonnes), and had two main masts. Its deck was 53 feet (16 meters) long and it was six feet, six inches (one meter, 98 centimeters) wide. The *Nonsuch* was purchased specially for the journey. The *Eaglet* was also a two-masted ketch, and was leased from the British Royal Navy.

(above) The cargo included wampum necklaces made from strings of small seashells. The Native peoples used wampum for trading.

Trading Cargo

Both ships were fully stocked before they left for their journey. They had to include enough food supplies for the men to survive a cold winter on the shores of Hudson Bay. It was also important to include enough goods for trading with the local Native peoples for beaver pelts when they arrived. Some of the trade items included metal hatchets and spears, tobacco, pistols, gunpowder, paper, ink, compasses, lanterns, ropes, **pitch**, and tar. They also brought clothing such as shirts, socks, mittens, and shoes.

Navigation

Sailors in the 1600s used several instruments to determine their position at sea. By the late 1600s, sailors used a cross-staff to find their latitude, or how far north or south they were from the Equator. The Equator runs around the middle of the Earth like an invisible belt. The cross-staff was a T-shaped tool that helped sailors determine latitude by measuring the distance between the sun or stars and the horizon.

(right) A navigator uses a cross-staff to determine his position at sea.

Crew

The *Nonsuch* and the *Eaglet* did not require large crews because they were small compared to other seafaring vessels of the time. Historians believe that the ships could have been handled by as few as eight people. In wartime, it was recommended that at least 35 men staff British Royal Navy ketches. There were eleven crew members onboard the *Nonsuch* for the Hudson Bay voyage. Captain Zachariah Gillam commanded the ship. Other crew members included Thomas Shepard, **chief mate**, James Tatnam, mate, and Pierre Romieux, the ship's surgeon. The surgeon was responsible for dressing wounds, cutting the crew's hair, and pulling rotten teeth.

(background) A replica of the Nonsuch was built in 1968 to celebrate the 300th anniversary of the Hudson's Bay Company in 1970. The ship sailed north from England to the Orkney Islands, then sailed west into the Hudson Strait.

Native Life

The Great Lakes peoples and the Eastern Woodlands peoples lived in eastern Canada before the arrival of Radisson and des Groseilliers.

Language Groups

The Great Lakes peoples spoke Iroquoian-based languages and the Eastern Woodlands peoples spoke Algonquian-based languages. There were many different **dialects** within each group, but they were similar enough that peoples within the same language group could usually understand each other.

(above) The Great Lakes peoples grew food crops of corn and squash.

(below) The Great Lakes peoples fished and hunted moose from birchbark canoes.

At the Lakes

The Great Lakes peoples lived in the region stretching from Lake Ontario to Georgian Bay. There were two **confederacies** within this territory: the Haudenosaunee, or Iroquois Confederacy and the Wendat, or Huron Confederacy. The two groups were enemies. The Iroquois Confederacy was originally made up of five nations: the Mohawk, Seneca, Cayuga, Onondaga, and Oneida. The Huron lived in clans, or family groups called the Bear, Cord, Rock, and Deer.

Sharing a Hearth

The Great Lakes peoples farmed, hunted, and fished. They traveled by foot and by canoe. Several families lived together in wooden buildings called longhouses. They made their clothes from deerskin.

In the Woodlands

The Eastern Woodlands peoples lived in the region stretching from the upper Great Lakes and around Hudson Bay, out to present-day Quebec, Ontario, and Manitoba. The Eastern Woodlands peoples included the Algonquin, Ojibwa, and Cree peoples. The Woodlands peoples hunted for game and fish, and gathered plants and other foods. They made their clothing from moose, caribou, and deerskin. Men and women dressed alike in tunics, leggings, and moccasins. In winter they wore fur robes.

On the Move

The Woodlands peoples were **semi-nomadic**, traveling from place to place in search of food as the seasons changed. They built temporary shelters called wigwams wherever they went. They traveled on foot and by canoe in summer, and used snowshoes and pulled their belongings on toboggans in winter.

(right) A bark scroll with Ojibwa writing.

(background) Wigwams were made by cutting poles from trees and arranging them in a cone shape. The cone was covered in bark, woven rush mats, or caribou hides.

Two Worlds Meet

The early fur trade of New France was dependent on the settlers' relationship with the Huron peoples. The relationship was valuable to both sides, as each desired the other's trade goods.

Birth of the *Coureurs de Bois*

The Iroquois' wars against the Huron eventually ended the trading relationship between the Huron and the French. This made way for the *coureurs de bois*, such as Radisson and des Groseilliers. These men lived among the Native peoples, hired them as guides, and relied on them to help bring furs to the French colony.

Life in the Woods

The *coureurs de bois* watched the Native peoples and learned invaluable survival techniques. The Native peoples also hunted the fur-bearing animals that the Europeans desired. Without the participation of the Native peoples, there would have been no fur trade in North America at all.

Trade Goods

The Europeans traded many different kinds of goods with the Native peoples, including firearms and ammunition. Guns had a great impact on the lives of Native peoples because they were much more lethal than their traditional bows and arrows. The Iroquois were well armed from their trading with the Dutch and English. Guns made it easier for the Iroquois to defeat the Huron in 1649.

(above) Firearms changed the lives of Native peoples.

(right) Native women prized the copper kettles that Europeans brought. They could be placed directly over a fire.

Conflict

Radisson and des Groseilliers traded and lived with many different Native peoples. Some of the peoples they met were the Ojibwa, Cree, Assiniboine, and Dakota. Radisson's journals show his complex views toward the Native peoples with whom he lived and depended on for survival. At times, he appears to be in awe of their cleverness and skills. In other passages, he writes as though he pities them and thinks he is superior to them.

(background) A Native chief holds a wampum necklace or belt. Wampum was used to record events and was later used as money.

A.Bobbett Sc

After the Expedition

Radisson and des Groseilliers sailed to Hudson Bay again in 1670. They worked for the Hudson's Bay Company for four years as fur traders. Over time, they felt undervalued, so they returned to the service of France.

Another Disappointment

Radisson and des Groseilliers established La Compagnie du Nord, a French merchant company, to rival the HBC in the fur trade. They sailed from France to Hudson Bay, where they encountered a group of English HBC traders. Radisson and des Groseilliers took over the English ship, stole their cargo of furs, and sailed to New France. The French authorities, who had not forgotten about their previous **defection** to the English, seized their cargo.

(above) A seal from the official HBC charter.

(below) Lower Fort Garry was a HBC trading post built in present-day Selkirk, Manitoba.

Retirement

The incident in New France caused des Groseilliers to end his fur-trading career. He returned to his Trois-Rivières **estate** to enjoy retirement from the business. Radisson, who still wanted to live the life of a fur trader, rejoined the HBC and worked for several more years.

The Native Peoples

The Native peoples of North America played a crucial role in the fur trade. They were important **allies** in the wars between the English and the French. They also taught the Europeans how to survive winters in the harsh climate of the North.

Explorers

Many noted explorers followed in the footsteps of Radisson and des Groseilliers. Pierre Gaultier de Varennes et de La Verendrye, Alexander MacKenzie, and Simon Fraser sought their own fortune in exploring for the fur trade. Like Radisson and des Groseilliers, they set out on foot and by canoe, expanding the fur trade across Canada and claiming new territory.

(background) Traders unload furs at a HBC trading post. By the late 1600s, the fur trade had become extremely profitable.

-1674-

La Compagnie du Nord is created.

-1696-

Des Groseilliers dies in Trois-Rivières.

-1710-

Radisson dies in England.

-1713-

The Treaty of Utrecht ends the battle for control over the HBC forts and returns them to the English.

The HBC

The Hudson's Bay Company had a profound impact on the fur trade. It eventually stretched from coast to coast and played an important role in the development of Canada as a nation.

HBC Trading Posts

Charles Fort, later called Rupert House, was the first HBC trading post. Other posts soon popped up, such as York Factory, Severn House, Fort Albany, and Moose Factory. From 1682 to 1712, the forts changed ownership many times as the French and the English battled for control. The Treaty of Utrecht forced the French to return the forts to the English.

(above) Snowshoes helped trappers to walk across deep snow and hunt in the winter.

(below) Native peoples exchange beaver pelts for goods at a HBC trading post.

The Nor'westers

The next major rival of the HBC was the North West Company, formed in 1793. They expanded the fur trade to the west coast. The rivalry ended when the two companies merged into one in 1821.

Made Beaver

Made Beaver, or MB, was currency for the fur trade. It referred to a high-quality adult beaver pelt. The tokens were invented by George Simpson Mctavish at Albany Fort in 1854. Made Beaver tokens were spent in HBC stores.

Life at the Post

The posts were made up of several buildings where the men lived and stored their furs and other supplies. Protective walls sometimes surrounded the posts. The men hunted and fished for food, and maintained vegetable gardens. Sometimes they traded or bought food from the Native peoples who visited the fort or lived nearby. Women were not allowed at the forts.

Keeping Good Order

The HBC posts were structured by rank. There were **officers** who were in charge of a group of men, or servants as they were sometimes called. There were also blacksmiths, surgeons, carpenters, and other tradesmen who participated in running the forts. Many men married Native women and had families with them. This was not encouraged by the HBC, but many officers allowed it.

(background) Fort Prince of Wales on Hudson Bay. The forts were often called "factories" because the traders who ran them were called "factors."

A Lasting Impression

The legacy of Radisson and des Groseilliers can still be seen today. The HBC, founded on their discoveries, is still in business. Other French explorers later claimed territory in the United States and developed the fur trade there.

The Foundation of Canada

The Hudson's Bay Company is one of the foundations on which modern Canada was built. In association with the North West Company, the HBC fur traders mapped out Canada from coast to coast. Three of their forts are now capital cities of Canadian provinces, including Victoria, British Columbia; Edmonton, Alberta; and Fort Garry, now called Winnipeg, Manitoba.

Changing Lives

The fur trade altered Native cultures that had existed for centuries. Aside from introducing guns and other trade goods, the Europeans brought unrest to the Native communities they depended on for survival. Missionaries converted the Native peoples to Christianity and forced them to stop practicing their own spiritual beliefs and traditions. European settlers eventually claimed most of the land in North America, leaving only pockets of land, called reservations, to the Native peoples.

(below) European diseases such as smallpox wiped out many Native populations. Unlike Europeans, the Native peoples did not have any immunity against these illnesses.

Namesakes

Namesakes of Radisson and des Groseilliers dot North American maps. There are towns named after Pierre-Esprit, such as Radisson, Quebec, and Radisson, Wisconsin. The city Portage La Prairie in the province of Manitoba was named by Radisson and des Groseilliers, after their portages, which means carrying a canoe to avoid rough water when traveling.

(background) The international chain of Radisson hotels is named after Pierre-Esprit Radisson. The chain started in 1903.

Radisson EMPIRE Radisson

Glossary

ally Someone who helps someone else do something

benefactor A person who gives money to a person, group, or cause

charter An official government document that acknowledges rights or power over something

chief mate A sailor who was in charge of others on a merchant ship

Christian A religion based in the belief of one god and the teachings of Jesus Christ

colony Territory that is ruled by another country or nation

confederacy A large grouping of different peoples

convert To change one's religion, faith, or beliefs

defect To turn to another country for support

dialect A language specific to one region

divert To change course

East India Company A British merchant company that had a trading monopoly over India and other British colonies from 1600 to 1898

estate Property that belongs to someone

five-nation A group of five peoples from different regions

flotilla A fleet or group of boats

habitant Settlers who came to New France to help farm the land for seigneurs, or landowners

hatchet A small hand-held ax

immunity Protection against something, usually a disease

investor Someone who supports something or someone by giving money

Jesuit An organization of Catholic priests who preached Christianity in the New World

merchant company A group of traders that pool their money and resources

mission A trip made to preach a religion to a group of people

monopoly Supreme control over something or a region, especially in trade

New England The colony established by the English in the 1600s on the east coast of the United States

New World North, South, and Central America

officer Someone who has authority over others

ordain To make someone a religious leader

pitch A sticky black substance that was used for waterproofing materials

ransom Money demanded for the release of a prisoner

salary A regular payment of money

semi-nomadic To move seasonally in search of food

Seven Years War A worldwide conflict between the French and English colonists that lasted from 1756 to 1763

traitor Someone who goes against his or her country

Treaty of Utrecht A series of documents, one of which formally granted Rupert's Land and other HBC territory to England

Index

1 2 3 4 5 6 7 8 9 0 Printed in the U.S.A. 5 4 3 2 1 0 9 8 7 6